The Church's Year

Unfolding the Mysteries of Christ

by
David W. Fagerberg

*All booklets are published thanks to the
generous support of the members of the
Catholic Truth Society*

CATHOLIC TRUTH SOCIETY
PUBLISHERS TO THE HOLY SEE

Contents

Why Have a Liturgical Year? 3
   Following in Christ's footsteps 4
   Constitution on the Sacred Liturgy 4
The Season of the Incarnation 7
   Advent 7
   The Nativity of our Lord 12
   Epiphany 17
The Season of the Paschal Mystery 21
   Lent 21
   Holy Week 28
   Easter and the fifty days 32
The Season of Pentecost and the Church 40
   Pentecost 40
   Ordinary Time 45
Seeing Jesus in His Friends 49
   Why saints? 49
   Our Holy Lady 54
Conclusion 59
Further Reading 61

All rights reserved. First published 2014 by The Incorporated Catholic Truth Society, 40-46 Harleyford Road London SE11 5AY Tel: 020 7640 0042 Fax: 020 7640 0046. © 2014 The Incorporated Catholic Truth Society.

ISBN 978 1 86082 894 2

Why Have a Liturgical Year?

Perhaps you have had the experience of standing on the seashore and throwing a stick out into the waves. The stick eventually works its way back to shore, but not quickly or directly. The stick is pushed to shore eventually, but only by riding the peaks and troughs of successive waves. To an impatient observer it can look as though the stick is barely moving forward at all, and instead is only rising and falling on cyclical waves. But in actual fact, the energy of the waves does move a small amount of water forward in each cycle, eventually bringing the stick back to land.

I would like to propose this as the image behind this booklet concerning the liturgical year. We may not pay close attention to the liturgical calendar because it is so predictable - indeed, a new one comes by every year! We tend to only remember exceptional individual days, like a Christmas Day from childhood or a special family Easter, while the whole year itself escapes our attention by its repetition. We have lived through so many Advents and Lents that we may not give them attention any more. Nevertheless, I propose that like that piece of driftwood moving forward on the cycle of rising and falling waves, our souls are carried forward, toward heaven, on cyclical liturgical seasons. Each liturgical year pushes us toward the shoreline where God awaits us. There is a swell to each liturgical season, and with each rising and falling we are moved a little bit forward.

Following in Christ's footsteps

The mysteries of Christ are unfolded across days, weeks, and seasons of the year so that we may be linked to them. A Benedictine monk named Blessed Columba Marmion expressed it this way: "What makes Christ's mysteries ours is, above all, because the Eternal Father saw us with his Son in each of the mysteries lived by Christ and because Christ accomplished them as Chief of the Church" (*Christ in His Mysteries*). In other words, the mysteries that we celebrate actually involve us in some way. Marmion says that Christ attaches a special grace to each of his mysteries in order to "help us to reproduce within ourselves His divine features in order to make us like unto Him." Each exposure to these mysteries therefore heals and strengthens us.

Constitution on the Sacred Liturgy

Here is how the Second Vatican Council describes what happens over the course of a liturgical year:

"The Church is conscious that it must celebrate the saving work of the divine Bridegroom by devoutly recalling it on certain days throughout the course of the year. …Within the cycle of a year, moreover, she unfolds the whole mystery of Christ. ...Recalling thus the mysteries of redemption, the Church opens to the faithful the riches of her Lord's powers and merits, so that these are in some way made present for all time, and the faithful are enabled to lay hold upon them and become filled with saving grace." (*Constitution on the Sacred Liturgy*, ¶102)

It is as though the mystery of Christ is so huge that we cannot take it in by one glance. In order to get a sense of the palace in which we are living, we have to walk around in it and explore each room. The whole mystery must be unfolded over the course of an entire year - and more than that, it must be done again the next year, and the next. In this way are we able to lay hold upon our Lord's powers and merits, and be filled with grace. The year belongs to the Church to do with as she sees fit, and she sees fit to use it for our healing and sanctification.

In another paragraph, this document says that we recall Christ's mysteries of redemption so that they are "in some way made present for all time, and the faithful are enabled to lay hold upon them and become filled with saving grace" (¶102). We are not holding an empty cocoon in our hands from which the butterfly has already flown away. Rather, the feast is like a receptacle that still contains the Lord's powers and merits so that we can lay hold of them and advance in holiness.

The liturgical year is not just a parade that goes by in front of our eyes. We are to step into that one, holy, catholic and apostolic parade ourselves. It sets our Christian activity to a rhythm, and gives us ample time to practice our soul craft. That is why we want to look at each season of the liturgical year in this booklet.

The Season of the Incarnation

It would be a mistake to treat the incarnation as just the "opening act", as though the real action takes place at the cross and resurrection. The mystery of our redemption includes four saving acts: incarnation, crucifixion, resurrection, and ascension. The incarnation is not just a gimmick to get Jesus on stage! Let us see how the Church has prepared for and celebrated this mystery.

Advent

We probably know that Advent is the beginning of the Church year, and the season before Christmas. But in order to fully appreciate its flavour, it is good to remember that the Latin word *adventus* does not mean something we start up, or initiate ourselves. *Adventus* means "a coming, an approach, an arrival." If you have ever been up since midnight in the cold darkness, alone, and seen the night crack before the sun's probing rays, you have seen the sun advent (come). And if you have seen the resurrection put its shoulder against the door of death and push, you will have seen Christ advent (come). He comes to his people to set them free.

This has already been accomplished, yet it will not be fully accomplished until the Last Judgement, at the general resurrection. In his letter to the Romans St Paul says that we are under the dominion of sin, law, wrath, death and the devil. Christ has already broken these chains when his victory march out of Hades blew the gates off their hinges, nevertheless we still await his *adventus* in glory. Therefore Advent celebrates both what has begun and what still awaits completion. Advent is a season on tiptoe, eagerly peering over the dark horizon of sin and death where we find ourselves - first we see Christ come in the flesh at Bethlehem, but we also look for him to come in glory from the heavenly Jerusalem where he now reigns.

What we pray for

You can hear this in the Collects for the season, the prayers at the beginning of Mass which are specific to the day. On the first Sunday of Advent we ask Almighty God to "grant your faithful…the resolve to run forth to meet your Christ. …So that, gathered at his right hand, they may be worthy to possess the heavenly kingdom." On the second Sunday we ask that "no earthly undertaking hinder those who set out in haste to meet your Son, but may our learning of heavenly wisdom gain us admittance to his company." The third Sunday's Collect calls God's attention to how his people "faithfully await the feast of the Lord's Nativity," and asks that they be enabled "to attain the joys of so great a salvation and to celebrate them always with solemn worship and glad rejoicing."

We are nearing the day. The pace quickens. From 17th to 23rd December the evening prayers of the Church include the O Antiphons: seven responses sung before the Magnificat at Vespers that rise in crescendo. Who is coming? For whom do we wait? What is his name? *O Sapientia* (O Wisdom), *O Adonai* (O Lord), *O Radix Jesse* (O Root of Jesse), *O Clavis David* (O Key of David), *O Oriens* (O Rising Sun), *O Rex Gentium* (O King of the Nations), and *O Emmanuel*.

The Collect of the feast of the Nativity itself, on 25th December, confesses that God gladdens us year by year as we wait in hope for our redemption. Then it unites Bethlehem and the heavenly Jerusalem. "Grant that, just as we joyfully welcome your only begotten Son as our Redeemer, we may also merit to face him confidently when he comes again as our Judge."

The Scripture we will hear

The lectionary contains the readings for all the liturgies of the year and, in order to open the treasures of the Bible more lavishly, it is divided into three cycles. Cycle A draws from Matthew, B from Mark, and C from Luke; John is spread throughout the year, but with a special concentration in Easter and Pentecost. Even though each cycle will draw from a particular Gospel, the structure of the four Sundays of Advent is similar.

The gospel reading for the first Sunday is a warning of judgement. As it was in the days of Noah, so it will be at the coming of the Son of Man; be watchful and alert because you do not know when the time will come; there will be signs in the heavens and the nations will be in dismay. A Christian must always remain watchful and attentive, a point Jesus makes repeatedly in his parables using servants, wedding banquets, wise and foolish virgins, etc. In Advent we are presented with the fact that he will call for a decision from us.

The gospel reading for the second Sunday of Advent brings John the Baptist on the scene. His voice cries for repentance because the kingdom is at hand; he is a messenger sent ahead to prepare the way; the Word of God came to John the son of Zechariah in the desert. On the third Sunday of Advent John continues to be the subject of the gospel reading, but the tone shifts to clarify that he is not the Messiah. He is the last prophet. He himself says his disciples should look for another because he's not the one; he came to testify to the light, but he is not the light; he baptises with water, but one is coming who will baptise with fire. An abbot of a monastery once said to me, "Religion is building a road for God to come to you on." We do not force God to come near - that is all grace - but we are not passive, either. We prepare. And John the Forerunner is a friend of the Bridegroom who teaches us how to prepare: "Repent."

The gospel reading for the fourth Sunday of Advent begins the story of Mary. In one year we hear the story from Joseph's point of view (Matthew), as he himself learns from the angel of the Lord how Mary became pregnant through the Holy Spirit; another year we hear the story from Mary's point of view (Luke), as the gospel tells us of Gabriel's announcement to her; and in the final year we learn of Mary's visit to Elizabeth, in whose womb John the Baptist leaps, and we smile at hearing a familiar refrain of the Hail Mary for the first time ("Blessed are you among women, and blessed is the fruit of your womb").

History and eschaton

The lectionary chooses the Old Testament lesson in conjunction with the gospel reading, so listen also for themes of anticipation and judgement in the Old Testament prophets. When Baruch tells Jerusalem to take off its robe of mourning and misery, it is both because the babe has been laid in the manger and because her children will be gathered from the east and the west. When Zephaniah tells Zion to shout for joy, it is because the Lord has removed the judgement against Zion and the King of Israel is in its midst. Micah is speaking to tiny Bethlehem when he says the Ruler of Israel will come from this city, and two verses later the greatness of this Ruler will reach to the ends of the earth, and he will bring peace.

These prophets mingle the historical *adventus* of Jesus to Bethlehem with the eschatological *adventus* of the Son of Man for whom we still wait.

This is put vividly in the Collect for the Vigil Mass of the Nativity. "O God, who gladden us year by year as we wait in hope for our redemption, grant that, just as we joyfully welcome your only begotten Son as our Redeemer, we may also merit to face him confidently when he comes again as our Judge." Advent arcs between the historical deeds of God and the final redemption. The arrival of Christ in history has turned the page to the final chapter of time.

The Nativity of our Lord

The Church rejoices over the arrival of Emmanuel at her Christ Mass (Christmas). Emmanuel means "God with us". A people who walked in darkness have seen a great light. Unto us a child is born, in the city of David, who is Christ the Lord. And the Collect for the Christmas Day Mass goes straight to the heart of its consequence: "O God, who wonderfully created the dignity of human nature and still more wonderfully restored it, grant, we pray, that we may share in the divinity of Christ, who humbled himself to share in our humanity."

The prayer indicates that this feast is more than just a birthday (though not less than that). It is celebrating the birth of Christ, true, but since Christ is the Son of God made man, his birth has special consequences. The Christmas feast concerns the dignity of human nature. God created that nature, different from the angels or the animals; sin has corrupted and damaged it; and in the birth of Christ it is being wonderfully restored. The incarnation is not just a way to get Jesus on stage; rather, the incarnation itself is a saving act because here divine nature is united with human nature in order to deliver it from corruption and death.

The tradition calls this "divinisation". God became man, and this opens the door for human beings to participate in God so intimately that they share his life: they are divinised. 2 Peter 1:4 explains it like this:

> "His divine power has bestowed on us everything that makes for life and devotion, through the knowledge of him who called us by his own glory and power. Through these, he has bestowed on us the precious and very great promises, so that through them you may come to share in the divine nature…"

In other words, what Christ is by nature, we are to become by grace!

The purpose of the incarnation

Divinisation certainly does not mean our nature changes from human to divine. We remain human beings, and do not become deities. One of the ways the Church fathers explained this was with an image of placing an iron rod into a fire. Iron is cool by its own nature, but when plunged into fire it participates in the fire's heat and becomes hot itself. This is professed in the *Catechism of the Catholic Church* at paragraph 460, which quotes 2 Peter: "The Word became flesh to make us *'partakers of the divine nature'*." And then the paragraph quotes Athanasius ("For the Son of God became man so that we might become God") and Thomas ("The only begotten Son of God, wanting to make us sharers in his divinity, assumed our nature, so that he, made man, might make men gods"). Christ has unified a divine and human nature in himself, so when we are plunged into him we become by grace what he is by nature. This mystery is confessed at every Eucharist, though quietly. During the preparation of the chalice, the priest or deacon adds water to the wine and says, "By the mystery of this water and wine may we come to share in the divinity of Christ who humbled himself to share in our humanity."

The importance of the incarnation

This is why the early Church councils found it so crucial to defend the fact that Jesus was fully human. If he did not share our entire nature, he could not heal the corruption sin has caused to soul, body, mind, will, and so forth. Gregory of Nazianzus made it short and sweet: "What is not assumed is not healed." Jesus had to assume our entire humanity. That is why the early Church councils refuted those who were known as gnostics. Gnostics thought that matter was fallen, and bodies were bad, and therefore Jesus could not have a real one. They denied a real incarnation, as if Jesus' humanity was pretend. The opening verse of one of the gnostic Gospels simply says that "In the fifteenth year of Tiberius Caesar… Jesus descended out of heaven into Capernaum, a city in Galilee, and began teaching in the synagogue."

How different are the Gospels we hear at the Christmas liturgies. Christmas is the only day on which three Masses may be celebrated, following an ancient tradition in Rome: Midnight, Dawn, and during the Day. And over the course of those liturgies we hear about the decree from Caesar Augustus, and no room at the inn, and having to put a newly swaddled babe in a manger. (A manger was the food trough where someone normally put grain for the animals to eat. The Eucharistic imagery of Christ, our bread of life, being placed in a manger was not lost on the early Church.)

Most of the ancient world was not particularly surprised by the idea of a god walking among men and women. This was sometimes done by Zeus, Hera, Athena, and others. But none of these "visits" is the same as the Christian doctrine of the incarnation. In those visits, the god took on the appearance of a human being, but did not become one. What was novel in Christianity, and startling to the pagan religious world, was the idea that God had truly become fully human. That is what the Nicene Creed is defending when it says, "For us men and for our salvation he came down from heaven, and by the Holy Spirit was incarnate of the Virgin Mary, and became man" (*incarnatus est de Spíritu Sancto ex María Vírgine*).

Why 25th December?

Even the selection of 25th December as the date for Christmas figures in here. Scholarship is not one hundred percent agreed on this, but many agree with the following thesis.

There was an expectation in the ancient world that an exceptionally holy person would die on the same date on which he was born. In other words, the holier a person was, the more complete and symmetrical was his or her life. By working backward through the calendars, the early Church concluded that the Passover had been on 25th March in the year when Jesus died. Then from what I've been saying, wouldn't it follow that Jesus came to earth on 25th March? He did! He became incarnate of the Virgin Mary on that date: it is the feast of the Annunciation. And he was born nine months later, on 25th December.

The sacredness and the joy of Christmas is marked with an octave, as is Easter. Christmas doesn't end as soon as all the presents have been opened: it is eight days long. How could we contemplate so great a mystery as Christ becoming man in only one day? When counting an octave, you include the day on which it began (e.g. if Christmas falls on Tuesday, the octave ends on Tuesday of the following week). Eight days after Christmas is 1st January, the Solemnity of Mary. We come full circle.

And because a fire warms to those who sit nearest to it, on the Sunday following Christmas we celebrate the feast of the Holy Family. Other days in the octave commemorate the spread of this warmth, some with costly consequence: 26th December is the feast of St Stephen, the first martyr; the 27th is the feast of St John, the apostle and evangelist; and the 28th is the feast of the Holy Innocents.

Christianity is the good news that God so loved the world that he became man, and that we may share in the divinity of Christ because he has humbled himself to share in our humanity. There is a divine exchange. Christmas means that the goal of our life is to become a saint: divinised.

Epiphany

According to the *Universal Norms for the Liturgical Year* the season of Christmas runs from the first evening prayer of Christmas until the Sunday after Epiphany. The normal date for Epiphany is 6th January, though it may be transferred to a Sunday. The "Twelve Days of Christmas" that you might know from the English carol are the twelve days between Christmas and Epiphany. The first Sunday that falls after 6th January is the feast of the Baptism of the Lord.

Sometimes you hear people say, "I've had an epiphany." I think they mean they have had a sudden realisation. However, the root of the word refers less to an idea in our minds, and has more to do with something appearing to us. *Phainein* means "to show, display, manifest". And *epi* means "upon", or coming from above. "Epiphany" means the striking appearance of something.

Alas, Christ's appearance in the world is all too easy to miss. Judaea was an insignificant country in the Roman empire; Jesus' neighbours dismissed him when he preached in their synagogue; he died abandoned by all but his mother and the beloved disciple. Not a very spectacular start. And yet the prayer for the vigil of the Epiphany says, "May the splendour of your majesty, O Lord, we pray, shed its light upon our hearts." The light of this splendour is not seen by all; it must be *epiphanised* by God, to be received by faith. And the ones to whom God reveals himself always seems to be surprising. Israel knew this from its own history. It was the least of the nations, yet chosen by God. And now, when the incarnate God has come to his people Israel, the ones who recognise him confound our expectations again.

Who meets Jesus on his arrival?

No official government delegation, either Roman or Israelite, was there to greet him. It is not King Herod at the foot of the manger. Indeed, had he sent a delegation, it would have been for nefarious reasons. The slaughter of the Holy Innocents, a feast that was originally connected with Epiphany (but now celebrated on the fourth day of the Christmas octave), proves that. Chesterton says it is perhaps undignified to think of the Creator being smuggled into his own creation, but the story about a king being born in a cave has that note about it.

"It is not only that the very horse-hoofs of Herod might in that sense have passed like thunder over the sunken head of Christ. It is also that there is in that image a true idea of an outpost, the piercing through the rock and an entrance into enemy territory. There is in this buried divinity an idea of undermining the world…" (*The Everlasting Man*)

Shepherds from the hillsides know that something is going on. Shepherds have always been favoured in the history of Israel. But more surprising guests arrive. Foreigners, strangers from beyond the borders of Israel. Yet to them the splendour of God's majesty, hidden in the cave, lures them by a star's leading light. These men were called magi because they were wise, and they were wise because they were watching for signs of God. The tradition later identified them as kings, because had not Psalm 72:11 said "May all kings fall down before him"? They bring gifts that have been interpreted as signs of Jesus' identity: "gold, as to a king; myrrh, as to one who was mortal; and incense, as to a God" (*Contra Celsus*, Origen).

The Gentiles come to do homage, and that is a sign that Jesus is Lord of all the nations. They had not been prepared for his arrival the way Israel had been, yet they came to honour him when they were called. May we hope to do as much. The prayer for the day of Epiphany says, "Grant in your mercy that we, who know you already by faith, may be brought to behold the beauty of your sublime glory."

Baptism of Jesus

On the Sunday after this is another epiphany of sorts: the baptism of Jesus in the Jordan. (In fact, the eastern Church celebrates this on Epiphany, while the western Church celebrates the coming of the magi.) Jesus' identity is revealed when the Father says "You are my beloved Son," and the Holy Spirit descends in bodily form like a dove. It is one of the few places in the New Testament where all three persons of the Trinity make an appearance together. Something more than John's baptism with water is about to be let loose over the face of the earth: no longer a watery baptism of repentance, but a fiery baptism of regeneration. So on this Sunday we pray, "Grant that your children by adoption, reborn of water and the Holy Spirit, may always be well pleasing to you." As Jesus sanctified every grave when he was laid in the tomb, so here he sanctifies every baptismal font by going down into the Jordan.

The Season of the Paschal Mystery

It is impossible to separate the cross and the resurrection. We create problems if we do. However, we are only able to think one thought at a time, so we must treat one first, and then the other. In this chapter we will lead up to the cross through Lent, and then lead away from the empty tomb through the fifty days of the Easter season. But know that it is a single journey. The two operations are united. A doctor performs the procedure of an appendectomy on his patient; the Divine Physician performs the procedure of cross and resurrection on us.

Lent

Lent is a paradoxical season. On the one hand, the word itself names something joyful: *lencten* in Old English means "springtime", because the days begin to lengthen. The dead of winter is behind us, and the grass will begin to show through the snow cover any day. On the other hand, Lent is a season of asceticism. The word *askesis* originally meant the kind of training or discipline that an athlete underwent. Then it was applied to spiritual self-discipline for the sake of training one's prayer life. One lifts weights at the gym to gain strength in the arm; Lenten asceticism is doing spiritual reps. It is the discipline required to become an icon of Christ, and make his image visible on our faces. The whole aim of the Lenten asceticism is to refresh our spiritual conformity to Christ.

Time and time again Israel's prophets spoke about the need to go back into the desert where Moses had led Israel's ancestors. This was a land between Egypt (which they had just left) and the Promised Land (to which they were still on their way). In this in-between-place Israel remembered God, relied only on God, listened more carefully to God. They were there for forty years. We are in Lent for forty days.

Lent originated as the final preparation by catechumens for their upcoming baptism at Easter. They had spent years in the first phase of their catechumenate, when they had been called "auditors" because they listened to the Word of God. They heard it in Scripture while attending the first half of the Mass (then called the liturgy of the catechumens), and they heard it in the life-instructions they were learning from their sponsors about prayer, fasting, and almsgiving. Now, at the beginning of the forty-day countdown to the font, they were enrolled by the Bishop by "giving in their name" to be written down by his own hand. They were chosen for baptism, so in the second phase of their catechumenate they were called "elect".

It is easy enough to see how the already-baptised would find it valuable to go back into that desert, too. And so do we. We return to the desert in order to remember God, rely on God, listen more carefully to God's promises. Lent is offered to us as a time to open our ears, soften our hearts, intensify our asceticism, refocus our charity. As the Collect for Ash Wednesday says, "Grant, O Lord, that we may begin with holy fasting this campaign of Christian service, so that, as we take up battle against spiritual evils, we may be armed with weapons of self-restraint." Ascetical training.

Fasting

Although the Church calls for an increase of all three Christian disciplines - prayer, fasting, and almsgiving - it is fasting that most people associate with Lent, so a word should be said about it. Just don't neglect the other two.

There are many reasons to fast, and with a little reflection you could think of as many as I could. People fast for health reasons (like when your cholesterol is too high), for medical reasons (like before a blood test), or for reasons of vanity (like the magazines encourage). But a liturgical fast is different. Its reason is given in Scripture: "Man shall not live by bread alone." Jesus recited this passage from Deuteronomy 8 during his fast in the desert.

In any kind of discipline we discover that we must deny ourselves temporary goods for a greater goal. The athlete gives up desserts to get in shape. In the liturgical case, we deny ourselves temporal goods for an eternal goal. There is nothing wrong with bread, but when tempted to turn stones into bread Jesus replied that there is a higher good. We restrain what we eat during Lent so that we can remember that higher good. The primary aim of fasting is to make us conscious of our dependence upon God.

Ash Wednesday

The number forty appears numerous times in Scripture, and seems to represent a time of testing or judgement. It is the length of time necessary to accomplish some major design by God.

It was for forty years that Israel ate manna in the desert, and it was for forty days that the rain fell in Noah's day, that Moses was on the mountain with God, and that the city of Nineveh had to repent. But the most influential scriptural example was the forty days that Jesus was tempted (this being the gospel lesson on the first Sunday of Lent in all three cycles). We follow our Lord into in the wilderness.

How did Lent come to begin on a Wednesday? A feast always trumps a fast, and Sunday is a feast. Therefore, Sundays are not counted, and six weeks times six days equals thirty-six; add four to reach Wednesday. (In the eastern Church neither the Sabbath nor Sunday are counted, so they have an eight-week Lent: five times eight.)

The Scripture for Ash Wednesday is the same in each lectionary cycle. The prophet Joel tells us *why* we are doing it, and in the Gospel of Matthew Jesus tells us *how* to do it. Even now, Joel proclaims - after we've failed in our resolve and fallen short of our intentions - if we return to him with our whole heart we will find him gracious and merciful. Lent begins with a prophetic announcement that God is "slow to anger, rich in kindness, and relenting in punishment." So gather the people, notify the congregation, assemble the elders and the children. Get a move on!

Then in the Beatitudes Jesus tells us how to fast. Do not be concerned with the impression you hope to make on other people. Go to your inner room, don't toot your own horn ("don't blow a trumpet before you when you give alms"), don't look gloomy while you fast. Anoint your head, wash your face, don't look like you're fasting. It is always jarring to hear this gospel just before a smear of ashes is put on our forehead but we are not receiving those ashes to show off, rather to join Job, Daniel, David and others in a sign of repentance, mourning and humility. We are being told to be concerned with our own hearts. Then our reward will not come in the form of admiration by others, we will be rewarded by the only one who can see what is hidden in our hearts, namely our Father.

The Scripture we will hear

The first Sunday of Lent tells us of Jesus' temptation, whether the readings are from Matthew, Mark or Luke (cycle A, B or C). It is paired with a different Old Testament reading in each cycle: the fall, the covenant with Noah, and the command to bring first fruits to the altar. The Old Testament reading of the second Sunday focuses on Abraham: his call, the terms of God's covenant with him, and the ratification of the covenant by sacrifice.

On the remaining three Sundays, the Old Testament readings tell familiar stories about redemption and covenant. In cycle A we hear about Israel grumbling in the wilderness, God's election of David as king, and Ezekiel's prophecy about old bones rising. In cycle B the Ten Commandments are repeated, the bronze serpent lifted up heals people from snake bites, and a new covenant will be written on a heart of flesh. Finally, in cycle C the prophet Isaiah wonders why we spend money on what is not real, Joshua celebrates a Passover before going into the Promised Land, and God promises Isaiah that he will do a new deed.

In two of the lectionary cycles (B and C), those Old Testament lessons are paired with gospel readings that line up along an axis pointing to Golgotha. Pressure is mounting. Jesus has set his face to go to Jerusalem and suffer, and when Peter objects he is called "a Satan." Jesus clears the temple; he will be lifted up on the cross to heal us because God so loved the world. The transfiguration on Mt Tabor is described, the prodigal son is welcomed back, and Judas objects to using expensive perfume to anoint Jesus' feet in anticipation of his burial.

However, cycle A of the lectionary is special. When there are catechumens for baptism at the coming Easter, they are to receive the scrutinies on the third, fourth and fifth Sundays of Lent. "The scrutinies…are rites of self-searching and repentance…and meant to uncover, then heal all that is weak or sinful in the hearts of the elect" (Rite of Christian Initiation of Adults, ¶141). In that case, the gospel readings from John are always used, no matter what cycle one is in for the rest of the year. These have strong baptismal themes: water, blindness and new life. They are the gospel accounts of the Samaritan woman at the well, the man born blind and the raising of Lazarus, and they are co-ordinated with the scrutiny of the catechumens on their home stretch.

Transition

The last week of Lent is Holy Week, and will begin with Palm Sunday. The day before Palm Sunday we pray to God to grant us "the grace to will and to do what you command, that the people called to eternal life may be one in the faith of their hearts…" If the season of Lenten asceticism has softened our hearts, then we will want to do what God commands and we will go into Holy Week as one people, with one faith and one hope.

Holy Week

We have reached the holiest week of the year, the celebration of our Lord's paschal mystery. The Greek word *pascha* corresponds directly to the Hebrew word *pesah*, which means "pass over". This word had already taken a double reference in Jewish tradition. It points us to (a) the angel of death *passing over* the households in Egypt marked by the blood of the lamb on the doorpost, and (b) the Israelites *passing through* the Red Sea to escape Pharaoh's soldiers. The Christian tradition inherited both. The blood of the Lamb of God causes death to *pass over* anyone who is marked with the sign of the cross at baptism and invited to join the household of the Church, and Christ descended into Hades to *pass through* death, bringing Adam and Eve (and us) out with him as he tramples Death by his death.

Its beginning: Palm Sunday

By the time we reach Palm Sunday we know what Jesus is in for, but to remind us, the Old Testament reading every year is Isaiah 50: he will give his back to those who beat it, his cheeks to those who pluck his beard, his face to those who want to strike it. Jesus' suffering on the cross is voluntary. He does it for us. This is what he has come to do, and he will not turn back from it even if abandoned by his most enthusiastic followers. As if to let us experience how quickly the crowd turned against Jesus, Palm Sunday turns on a dime in its mood. At the very beginning of Mass we hear the account of

Christ's joyful entry into Jerusalem amid cheering crowds, but by the time we reach the gospel at its normal place in the liturgy we hear how it all turns out. Betrayal, false trial, Pilate, torture, mockery, death. The Collect invites us to imitate Christ's suffering and death. "Almighty ever-living God, who as an example of humility for the human race to follow caused our saviour to take flesh and submit to the cross, graciously grant that we may heed his lesson of patient suffering and so merit a share in his resurrection."

Its conclusion: the Triduum

Israel knew that the sacrifices of the temple had opened up a communion with Yahweh. The Church knew that Christ had opened up a yet fuller communion because of who he was, so sacrifice was used to explain the death on the cross. Sacrifice involves three stages: offering, immolation and acceptance. In the Old Covenant a priest must offer the lamb, it was killed and then it was accepted by God. In the New Covenant, Christ is our high priest and he made the offering on Maundy Thursday; Christ is the victim and he was killed on Good Friday; and the Father showed his acceptance of the Son's sacrifice by raising him from the dead on Easter Sunday. This full sacrifice is celebrated at every Sunday Mass, it is true, but in the Easter Triduum we break it down. Although we attend three services, the Triduum may be considered one liturgical day, unfolding the unity of Christ's paschal mystery for us over three days.

Maundy Thursday

Thursday of Holy Week is called Maundy Thursday because the Latin word *mandatum* means commandment: "A new commandment I give to you, that you love one another" (John 13). With this command the Church receives its lifeblood. The Son was the sacrament of the Father's love (when someone encountered Christ, they encountered the Father's love), and the Church is to be the sacrament of Christ's love (someone can encounter Christ in his Church). The posture and identity of the Church in the world is revealed twofold on Thursday. First, the Gospel of John records Jesus washing his disciples' feet, and if he has washed our feet, we ought to wash one another's. Second, the other three Gospels record Jesus' command, "Do this." Do what? The thing he has just done: he offered his sacrificial death to the Father. The posture of the Church in the world is one of servant washing feet, and the identity of the Church in the world is a priest mediating between God and humanity. Because the Last Supper has been understood to be the establishment of the priesthood, priests and deacons of the diocese renew their priestly promises to the Bishop when they gather on Thursday afternoon for the chrism Mass.

The Mass of the Lord's Supper is in the evening, but this is less because we are trying to mimic a historical detail, and more in order to begin the three great days. In Jewish tradition, a day begins at sunset. So the Church gathers "to participate in this most sacred Supper," which Christ entrusted to the Church "when about to hand himself over to death," so that "we may draw from so great a mystery, the fullness of charity and of life" (Collect for Maundy Thursday). Feet are washed, again not so much to mimic a historical detail (this is not a passion play), but so that the Church may herself do as Christ did. At the liturgy's close, the most Blessed Sacrament is transferred from the altar of sacrifice to the altar of repose, and the faithful are invited to continue adoration into the night.

Good Friday

Friday of the Passion of the Lord consists of three parts: liturgy of the word, adoration of the cross and holy communion. The bare altar keeps us aware of the suffering our Lord underwent for us, who "by the shedding of his blood, established the paschal mystery" (Collect for Good Friday). The Church prays solemn intercessions for (i) herself, (ii) the Pope, (iii) the ordained and faithful, (iv) catechumens, (v) the unity of Christians, (vi) the Jewish people, (vii) those who do not believe in Christ, (viii) those who do not believe in God, (ix) those in public office and (x) those in tribulation. You can sense the attention of the Church expanding outward, in increasing circles of charity, like rings from a stone thrown into a pond. Next there is an adoration of the holy cross, worshipped with an appropriate gesture such as a genuflection or a kiss, and then comes an abrupt communion. There is no Eucharistic prayer at this liturgy, the only day of the year in which there is not one. No Eucharistic sacrifice is made, but we pray the Our Father and receive the body of Christ that was consecrated at the Thursday liturgy.

On Holy Saturday the Church vigils. She "waits at the Lord's tomb in prayer and fasting" (rubrics concluding Friday liturgy). Then the dawn of the resurrection begins to break.

Easter and the fifty days

A traditional way of reading Scripture is called "typology". It ties a connection between a type and its fulfilment, a shadow and its body. If a person approached a room with a bright light behind him, his shadow would enter the room before he did. When Christ approached humankind, his shadows (types) entered history before he did physically. Before he was born in Bethlehem, he was foreshadowed in events in the history of Israel. That is why Augustine said the New Testament is hidden in the Old Testament, and the Old Testament is fulfilled in the New. These types (shadows) can help flesh out Christ's full identity. For example, what would it mean to call Jesus the "Lamb of God" if we did not know the story of the sacrificed Passover lamb whose blood protected the inhabitants of a house? Or, how could we understand what it means for the catechumen to pass through the font if we did not know about Israel's miraculous escape through the water?

The Scripture we will hear

The Easter Vigil capitalises on this typology in two places. First, in the Scripture reading for the night. The Easter Vigil readings are not three, like an ordinary Mass, but nine (though for pastoral reasons it may be reduced to six). Jesus is the hinge holding these two folios together. "O God, who by the pages of both Testaments instruct and prepare us to celebrate the paschal mystery…" (prayer following the last Old Testament lesson).

In the record of these veiled foreshadowings, God has paced off the boundaries of salvation history that awaited its fulfilment in Jesus Christ. The vigil proclaims the story of creation, Abraham's sacrifice of Isaac, Israel's exodus through the Red Sea, two prophecies by Isaiah about God's tenderness (his willingness to take us back, and calling the thirsty to water), Baruch's instruction to stay near the fountain of wisdom, and God's promise through Ezekiel to give us a new heart and new spirit. Then is proclaimed Paul's profound statement to the Romans about being baptised into Christ's death, followed by the gospel account of the resurrection by Matthew, Mark or Luke, according to the year's cycle.

The second place the Easter Vigil capitalises on typology is in the prayer blessing the water in the font. In baptism, water signifies tomb, womb and cleansing. The prayer names times that water has been used sacramentally by God to kill sin, to bring life and to regenerate: creation, the flood, the Red Sea, John in the Jordan and water from the side of Christ on the cross. It is as if the sacrament was saying that if someone was not there on the first occasion, this font will become for them a miniature flood to drown their sins, a miniature Red Sea that leads to freedom, an eddy of the Jordan where Christ was baptised and the water from where Christ himself was pierced.

What we pray for

Scripture and sacrament together accomplish what we ask for in the Collect: "stir up in your Church a spirit of adoption, so that, renewed in body and mind, we may render you undivided service." The word "adoption" is another of the keywords for divinisation in the *Catholic Catechism*, along with "supernatural life", "union", "communion", "eternal life", and "sanctification". Out of the mystery celebrated on this night Christians are reborn, made new persons, refreshed and redeemed. No wonder the Church has an instinct to gather on this holy night, and no wonder it was one of the favoured days for baptism.

The baptism of catechumens happens between the Liturgy of the Word and Eucharist. The water is blessed, as described above; the priest may plunge a candle into the font (Christ is candle, Spirit is flame, water is regenerated Church); the baptised receive the marks of their identity: oil, fire and the white garment. With the Bishop's permission, adults who have been baptised receive the sacrament of confirmation at the hand of the priest.

Then all renew their baptismal promises. "Do you renounce Satan, his works, and his empty show?" This last refers to a procession the Greeks called *pompa*, in which an idol was carried in a circular procession around the city. The Church fathers saw this as Satan marching his *pompa* around the world, but at baptism one more person drops out of the parade. And then the priest puts to the assembly the questions of the Apostles' Creed. "Do you believe in God, the Father…Do you believe in Jesus Christ…Do you believe in the Holy Spirit?" The Nicene Creed came out of the Ecumenical Council of Nicaea in 325, but the Apostles' Creed - shorter, blunter, more intimate - likely came from this baptismal setting. By the new birth which comes from water and the Holy Spirit we are adopted and divinised, and as children of God we go to the table of the Lord.

The octave of Easter

As at Christmas, we cannot absorb all this in an hour, or even a long night: we need an octave. The number eight is significant, and was not chosen at random. The Jewish people numbered the days of their week, instead of giving them names. The week began on "the first day," Sunday, and ended on "the seventh day," Saturday. The seventh day, of course, was the Sabbath, the day God rested according to the book of Genesis, and so all of Israel rested with him. There was no rest while they were slaves in Egypt, so leisure on the Sabbath points not only to creation but also to freedom.

In six days God created, and on the seventh he rested, but God had to act again when humanity fell into sin. A creation that God himself had described as "very good" in Genesis 1 became corrupted in Genesis 3. Therefore, after the seventh day God did a further work: it was an eighth day. And this is the day of the resurrection. It is the day of restoration that has begun but is still developing. It is an eschatological day. The world is no longer ruled by the seven-day cyclical week because the future age has already broken into it. Jean Danielou writes, "the whole theology of Sunday is now seen clearly; it is the cosmic day of creation, the biblical day of circumcision, the evangelical day of the resurrection, the Church's day of the Eucharistic celebration, and, finally, the eschatological day of the age to come" (*Bible and the Liturgy*).

Christians are baptised into that eighth-day existence and for that reason many fonts were octagonal. Also, the newly baptised extended their celebration over eight days: they wore their white garment and did not wash off their chrism oil until the octave was over. It was called "the Shining Week". The Collects for daily Mass during the octave speak of God giving constant increase to his Church by new offspring, of heavenly gifts and perfect freedom, of meriting to reach eternal joys, of many nations being one in faith, of reconciling the human race in the paschal covenant and of being clothed with immortality.

The fifty days of Easter

This is still not enough time to celebrate the paschal mystery. Easter is one day, Easter is eight days, Easter is fifty days. The paschal candle remains in place during this season, and it is common to celebrate the sprinkling rite on Sundays. The *Universal Norms for the Liturgical Year* says "the fifty days from Easter Sunday to Pentecost are celebrated in joyful exultation as one feast day, or better as one 'great Sunday'" (¶22). It ends on Pentecost - the fiftieth day. The Church seems to have the right proportionality: forty days of Lenten fasting and fifty days of Easter feasting.

What are we celebrating? Is there any better word to name it than "mercy"? In 2000 John Paul II designated the Sunday after Easter as the Sunday of the Divine Mercy (*divina misericordia*). The Collect rejoices that the recurrence of the paschal feast has kindled the faith of the people God made his own, and prays that "all may grasp and rightly understand in what font they have been washed, by whose Spirit they have been reborn, by whose blood they have been redeemed." This is the time for mystagogy with the newly baptised. They need to understand in what mystery they were plunged, and so do we all.

Who better to explain it to us than John the Theologian? The writer of the fourth Gospel is so named for his purity of life. At the Last Supper he laid himself upon Jesus, he stayed faithful at the foot of the cross and received Mary as his own mother. And so we hear from him extensively during the fifty days of Easter. The disciples were in a locked room and Jesus came among them, Thomas wasn't there so Jesus made a repeat appearance for his sake, Jesus came to the disciples while they were fishing and then had breakfast with them on the shore, he revealed the Father's name, he is the Good Shepherd, he is the vine and we are the branches, he has made our joy complete, he promises us the Advocate.

Feast of the Ascension

On the fortieth day the Church celebrates the feast of the Ascension of Jesus into heaven. I tried to stress earlier that the incarnation was not just a way to bring Jesus onstage, and I would like to insist as adamantly here that the ascension is not just a way to get him offstage. At the incarnation, the Son of God took human flesh from Mary and he keeps it. Jesus does not appear in costume and he does not take off his humanity at the ascension. The whole Christ, divine and human, ascends to sit at the right hand of the Father.

Thomas was surprised and didn't believe it until he put his finger in the nail holes. The Church fathers speculated that the angels were no less surprised. Irenaeus, Gregory of Nyssa, Ambrose, and more, describe the angels not recognising Christ as he nears heaven. The earthly angels cry out, "Lift up your gates and the King of Glory will enter." But the heavenly angels reply, "Who is this King of Glory?" (Psalm 24). Gregory Nazianzen summarises what should be the reply to those angels and to us.

> "Reply to those who doubt because of his body and the marks of his suffering which he did not have when he descended...Tell them that it is the Lord strong and mighty...Show them the beautiful tunic of the body which suffered and how it has grown even more beautiful in his passion."

But there is more. Jesus' ascent is not an escape route for him; it is a path blazed for us. This is the future of all who have been bound up with his life in love. We will be transfigured in the twinkling of an eye. Our destination is also the heavenly Jerusalem where the Lamb is now enthroned. God descended, man ascends. God became man so that man might be made divine. The Eternal Son entered our world so that we might enter the life of the Trinity. The ascension is the closing parenthesis to the incarnation which began everything. If we celebrate the beginning of the story, we should celebrate its end no less enthusiastically, so I am in favour of Ascension trees, Ascension cards and Ascension presents!

The Season of Pentecost and the Church

We could have placed Pentecost at the end of the last chapter, since "the period of fifty days ends on Pentecost Sunday" (*Universal Norms*). Indeed, the word means "fiftieth day", and was already called this by the Jews who were counting the days after their Passover. Thus the book of Acts of the Apostles can call it by that name in chapter 2, even before the tongues of fire appear: "When the day of Pentecost had come, they were all together in one place." But we have chosen to place it at the head of a new chapter so that we can discuss the Church, which was born on the day of Pentecost. This will also give us a chance to mention the two seasons of Ordinary Time in the year.

Pentecost

It is certainly true that original sin has an effect on each of us as individual persons. But the Church fathers also saw an effect of original sin upon mankind in total. Benedict XVI writes, "The essence of original sin is the split into individuality, which knows only itself. The essence of redemption is the mending of the shattered image of God, the union of the human race through and in the One who stands for all and in whom, as Paul says (*Ga* 3:29), all are one: Jesus Christ" (*Principles of Catholic Theology*).

Cyril of Alexandria says, "Satan has broken us up." The human race is now like a mirror that has been dropped on the floor into a thousand shards. But Augustine points out the remedy: "Divine Mercy gathered up the fragments from every side, forged them in the fire of love and welded into one what had been broken." Augustine has just described salvation history. All of it.

Undoing our babbling

You're probably aware that the first eleven chapters of Genesis have a different quality to them because they are a pre-history more than a history. They are like the beginning of the *Star Wars* movies when that slanted text floats by on the screen saying "In a galaxy far, far away…" In our case, too, we begin in the middle of a story and we want a word about our beginning: where did we come from, why were we created and why do we feel alienated from God? What happened? Things don't seem right; why not?

Genesis 1-11 answers that question with four stories that each have a three-step cycle. The cycle consists of sin, judgement and an act of mercy by God. The first story concerns Adam and Eve where the sin is disobedience, the judgement is pronounced and the act of mercy is exile from the garden lest they become fixed in their alienation forever. The second story concerns Cain and Abel where the sin is the first fratricide, the judgement is Cain being sent away and the act of mercy is the mark Yahweh puts on Cain indicating that no matter where he travels Yahweh will remain his God. The third story concerns Noah and the flood where the sin is a wickedness that has spread over the earth, the judgement is the flood which purified and the act of mercy is the ark, the rainbow and the covenant. The fourth story is the Tower of Babel where the sin is pride, and the judgement is "We will confuse their language and scatter them over the earth." But now comes a surprise. In the first three stories we have had sin, judgement and mercy, but in this story there is no third moment mentioned.

But wait. There *is* an act of mercy, after all. It is Genesis 12. It is Abraham, the father of Israel. It is the beginning of salvation history, the story of God creating a nation through which the Messiah will come to redeem the nations. The act of mercy is the entire economy of salvation - stretching from Abraham and the patriarchs, through slavery in Egypt, Moses and the exodus, the judges, the kings, the prophets and Jesus, right up to the establishment of the Church.

Pentecost reverses the Tower of Babel

At Babel people of one language were scattered into disparate nations; at Pentecost, people from the major nations of the world come to Jerusalem and discover they can understand the good news preached by the apostles. (That's why we read that tongue-tangling list from the book of Acts.) The fractured human race is reunited.

Pentecost reverses the effects of sin and that means (a) reconciliation with God and (b) unity with one another. In her catholicity the Church is a sign and instrument (i.e. a sacrament) of reunified humanity. The Church was already catholic because the twelve apostles (Matthias had replaced Judas) formed the twelve pillars of a new Israel that was destined to go to the corners of the world. It is not a Church for Jews or Gentiles only, for males or females only, for slave or free only (*Ga* 3:28); it is not a Church for one clan, or tribe, or kin, or ethnic group, or country. It is a universal Church.

The Collect reads:

"O God, who by the mystery of today's great feast sanctify your whole Church in every people and nation, pour out, we pray, the gifts of the Holy Spirit across the face of the earth and, with the divine grace that was at work when the gospel was first proclaimed, fill now once more the hearts of believers."

The face of the earth had been darkened in distrust and alienation and resentment as the fruits of sin; now the fruits of divine grace will begin to pour forth - like an artesian well that fills the canals running in every direction. Evangelisation has begun.

Other feasts nearby

The first Sunday after Pentecost is the solemnity of the Holy Trinity. (Since all three persons have now made their appearance, it is fitting to celebrate their mystery *in toto*.) That is followed by the solemnity of Corpus Christi (on Thursday or the next Sunday) because the Church receives her nourishment from the body and blood of her Lord. Nineteen days later is the solemnity of the Sacred Heart, and then the memorial of the Immaculate Heart of Mary. It is as if feasts that reveal the intimacies of our life in Christ crowd themselves around Pentecost.

The Scripture we will hear

In his sermon on that Pentecost day Peter quotes the prophet Joel who said God will pour out his Spirit upon all flesh in the last days. It is the beginning of the end; it is the age of the Church. This is paired with different gospel lessons so that over the three-year cycle we remember how Christ laid the foundation of the Church. We hear again on the fiftieth day, as we did on the first day of the Easter season, how Jesus appeared to his disciples in the locked room and breathed upon them the Holy Spirit. We hear him declare that rivers of living water flow from him. We hear his promise to send the Advocate. All of these come from the Gospel of John; all of these describe the Church as the mystical body of Christ.

St Paul uses the phrase "in Christ" (*en Christo*) 164 times in his writings. For example, "consider yourselves alive to God in Christ Jesus" (*Rm* 6:11), "if anyone is in

Christ, he is a new creation" (*2 Co* 5:17) and "have this mind among yourselves, which is yours in Christ Jesus" (*Phm* 2:5). We abide in Jesus and he abides in us, and this is made possible by the Holy Spirit. The Church is not the Jesus club. We do not create the Church. She is a divine product and she was in the mind of God from the beginning. The *Catechism of the Catholic Church* concurs with the Shepherd of Hermas when he says, "The world was created for the sake of the Church." What does this mean? The *Catechism* answers, "God created the world for the sake of communion with his divine life, a communion brought about by the 'convocation' of men in Christ, and this 'convocation' is the Church" (¶760).

Ordinary Time

This communion with God's divine life is the daily existence of the baptised Christian. It is celebrated by solemnities like Christmas and Easter, but everyone knows that a celebration does not mean the ordinary days are unimportant. I might celebrate my anniversary with an extra fancy dinner, but that doesn't mean I don't love my wife the other 364 days of the year. Liturgy expresses something that should be the basic stance of every moment of our lives and that's what the word "ordinary" means in this case, not tedious or boring, which we sometimes associate with the word. The Latin was *tempus per annum*: literally, "time through the year". That is ordinary which belongs to the usual order or course: customary, regular, usual.

It is related to *ordinal*, which means "counted time". These are the Sundays with numbers for names: Fifth Sunday of Ordinary Time, Twenty-seventh Sunday, etc. There are two blocks of Ordinary Time in the liturgical calendar. One follows the Christmas cycle (basically from the Baptism of the Lord, which takes the place of the First Sunday of Ordinary Time, until Ash Wednesday). The other follows the Easter cycle (basically from Pentecost all the way up to Advent of the next year). You can recognise them by their liturgical colour of green.

It's not as if these "ordinary Sundays" lack the mystery of Christ. The *Universal Norm* says:

> "Apart from those seasons having their own distinctive character, thirty-three or thirty-four weeks remain in the yearly cycle that do not celebrate a specific aspect of the mystery of Christ. Rather, especially on the Sundays, they are devoted to the mystery of Christ in all its aspects. This period is known as Ordinary Time" (¶43).

These Sundays don't break the mystery of Christ into smaller pieces, they serve it up whole.

Shine light through a prism and it is broken apart into a rainbow of reds and oranges and blues, but all those colours are in the white light. Shine the mystery of Christ through feasts and it is broken apart into Christmas and Easter and Pentecost, but all the aspects of Christ's mystery are in the Sundays of Ordinary Time.

The resurrection life is celebrated on every Sunday, which led Aidan Kavanagh to say that "Sunday is not a small Easter, rather Easter is a big Sunday." What we do every Sunday, we do in a big way at Easter. But we live from the fragrance of Christ's resurrected flesh all year long.

The Scripture we will hear

The readings for these Sundays tend to be semi-continuous readings through certain sections of Scripture, especially through Matthew, Mark and Luke. Large portions of each Gospel are read and you can watch the chapters go by from one Sunday to the next. The calendar was revised from a one-year cycle to a three-year cycle in order to fulfil the desire of the Second Vatican Council:

> "The treasures of the Bible are to be opened up more lavishly, so that richer fare may be provided for the faithful at the table of God's Word. In this way a more representative portion of the Holy Scriptures will be read to the people in the course of a prescribed number of years" (*The Constitution on the Sacred Liturgy*, ¶51).

Ordinary Time is an opportunity to put the teaching of Jesus in context and follow the thought through to the end.

The Old Testament lesson is selected to be congruent with the gospel reading.

And where does it lead us? To Christ, our King. The liturgical year ends with the solemnity of Christ the King. He is enthroned in our hearts as well as in heaven, in order to do his Father's will and restore all things. "We pray that the whole creation, set free from slavery, may render your majesty service and ceaselessly proclaim your praise" (Collect for Christ the King). We tumble through repeated liturgical years like a stone in a rock polisher, being smoothed and brightened by our contact with the mysteries.

Seeing Jesus in His Friends

Remove the back of your watch and you would see cogged wheels each moving in their own rotation but interconnecting at points. Open the liturgical year and you will find more than one organisation of time moving by its own logic but interconnecting at points.

The major division is between the temporal cycle and the sanctoral cycle. The temporal cycle is what we have described thus far: the seasons that annually commemorate different aspects of our Lord's life. The sanctoral cycle is our topic now. It consists of commemorations of events in the life of Christ and Our Lady, the lives of saints, and mysteries of our faith (events, persons, doctrines). These celebrations are arranged in a hierarchy of significance.

Why saints?

The *Catechism* answers that question this way:

> "By keeping the memorials of the saints - first of all the holy Mother of God, then the apostles, the martyrs and other saints - on fixed days of the liturgical year, the Church on earth shows that she is united with the liturgy of heaven. She gives glory to Christ for having accomplished his salvation in his

glorified members; their example encourages her on her way to the Father" (¶1195).

Three facts stand out from this. Firstly, salvation is by Christ's grace. We are honouring the saint for what Christ has done in him or her. The saint relates to Christ as the moon relates to the sun: it reflects another's light. Secondly, since death has been trampled down, the Church militant (we on earth) and the Church triumphant (those in heaven) are not isolated from each other. By keeping their day we put ourselves in the environs of heaven, being united with the liturgy of the saints, martyrs and angels. Thirdly, the saints are to be examples that encourage us. Their sanctity should not scare us off, but should draw us closer to ever greater intimacy with God.

There is more variety in heaven than in hell. Sin is a monotonous grey, but sanctity is a sparkling array of persons who are fully alive. Karl Adam writes, "How exceedingly various are the ways by which [the saints] followed Christ, and how manifold their forms of saintliness!" He then contrasts a series: the saintly hermit with the social saint of the great city, the saint in robes of penance with the refined saint of the salon, the saint of divine learning with the saint who despised all knowledge, the saint doing penance in rags with the saint robed in imperial purple. So he concludes, "How infinitely various are all the saintly figures. Each one is marked with a stamp of his own time, some very plainly so. ...For there is but One who is ever modern, never out of date, One only who belongs to all time" (*The Spirit of Catholicism*).

Does the Church call everyone to be alike? Yes, if you mean Christ-like. But the answer is really "No," because each will be Christ-like in his or her own, unique way. Do you want the same for each of your children? Of course: happiness. Do you want each of your children to be the same? Of course not: each is different. Each saint is different, made up of a unique personality that God brings to perfection.

God does not compare. He doesn't compare you to any other of his children but wishes to bring your unique personhood to fullness. The variety of saints reminds us of this. In each saint's life we see the hand of God sculpting them with a tool that God might also use upon us.

The hierarchy of feasts

1. *Solemnities.* This is the highest rank, and reserved for the most important mysteries of faith. Here are the fixed ones in chronological order: Solemnity of Mary the Holy Mother of God, the Epiphany of the Lord (January), St Joseph, the Annunciation of the Lord (March), the Nativity of St John the Baptist, Sts Peter and Paul, the Most Sacred Heart of Jesus (June), the Assumption of the Blessed Virgin Mary (August), All Saints (November), the Immaculate Conception, and the Nativity of the Lord (December). Here

are solemnities that are not always on the same date due to Easter moving from year to year: the Resurrection of our Lord, Ascension, Pentecost, Trinity Sunday, the Most Holy Body and Blood of Christ, the Most Sacred Heart of Jesus, Our Lord Jesus Christ King of the Universe. A solemnity will have the basic elements of a Sunday liturgy, no matter what day it falls on: three readings, Gloria, creed, etc.

2. *Feasts*. It is common to use the word "feast" to designate all three categories, but it also names technically a second rank. They are major celebrations related to Mary, apostles, Evangelists, some early martyrs and the archangels. Here they are in chronological order: the Baptism of the Lord, the Conversion of St Paul (January), the Presentation of the Lord, the Chair of St Peter the Apostle (February), St Mark (April), Sts Philip and James, St Matthias, the Visitation of the Blessed Virgin Mary (May), St Thomas, St James (July), the Transfiguration of the Lord, St Lawrence, St Bartholomew (August), the Nativity Of the Blessed Virgin Mary, the Exaltation of the Holy Cross, St Matthew, Sts Michael-Gabriel-Rafael (September), St Luke, Sts Simon and Jude (October), the Dedication of the Lateran Basilica, St Andrew (November), St Stephen, St John, the Holy Innocents, the Holy Family (December).

3. *Memorials*. These are too numerous to list. Some of them are obligatory, some are not. They are predominantly saints' days, e.g. Anthony, Athanasius, Thomas Aquinas,

Catherine of Siena, etc., but since Mary figures at the head of the saints, many memorials concern her: the Immaculate Heart of the Blessed Virgin, Our Lady of Sorrows, the Queenship of Mary, Our Lady of the Rosary, the Presentation of the Blessed Virgin Mary.

Canonising saints

In his letters, the apostle Paul speaks as if all members of the Church are saints. He addresses himself "to the saints [holy ones] who are in Ephesus" and in Colossae; the collection he takes up is to aid the saints in Jerusalem; he wants to equip the saints for the work of ministry. In this sense, every baptised person freed from sin can be considered a saint. However, when the Church has recognised a special holiness in certain men and women, has experienced the fact that they pray for us and wishes to honour them in memory, then that person is put on a canon (list). They are canonised. They are named as now being in heavenly glory, and may be publicly invoked and mentioned in the liturgy of the Church.

For the first millennium this was done locally. A particular church knew the exemplary holiness of a person, and was persuaded that this person interceded with Christ for them. They identified that person as a local saint. However, when a person's sanctity was honoured more widely, then his or her catholic (universal) character meant that their canonisation was overseen by the Pope.

They are inscribed in the General Calendar if they have universal importance and are celebrated throughout the whole Church.

Our Holy Lady

Mary stands in a unique position among the saints. She is the archetype of what we are all called to become. Being *Mater Dei* (Mother of God), she is also *Mater ecclesiae* (Mother of the Church). She has something in common with all her children, so she is named queen of patriarchs, prophets, apostles, martyrs, confessors, virgins and all saints. She is also the mother of every one of us. Louis Bouyer's expression is that Mary is not an unheard of exception, she is the masterpiece of grace. Therefore "she is…the living image, present within time, of what will be brought about in us all only at the end of time. …She is yet the image of what we have to become…" (*The Seat of Wisdom*)

In other words, what God did for her as a masterpiece of his grace, he would like also to do for us as members of his Son's mystical body. John Paul II says the same thing in his encyclical *Redemptoris Mater*. "The Church journeys through time toward the consummation of the ages, and goes to meet the Lord who comes. But on this journey…she proceeds along the path already trodden by the Virgin Mary" (¶2). Mary, then, does not receive these mysteries for herself, privately. All of her mysteries enable her to co-operate in God's divine activity which is directed at saving us. Though we haven't space to consider all of her mysteries, we might look at her three solemnities in this light.

Immaculate Conception (8th December)

Look at how the Collect of the day connects us to Our Lady. What we remember about her, we ask for ourselves:

> "O God, who by the immaculate conception of the Blessed Virgin prepared a worthy dwelling for your Son, grant, we pray, that, as you preserve her from every stain by virtue of the death of your Son, which you foresaw, so, through her intercession, we, too, may be cleansed and admitted to your presence."

God prepared a way. The *Catechism* says that because the Holy Spirit had prepared Mary, the Father found the dwelling place for the first time in the plan of salvation where his Son and his Spirit could dwell among men (¶721). It is just as necessary that God's Spirit prepare us for his indwelling. It is his hand that leads us to baptism and our membership in the mystical body of Christ.

Both Mary and we are saved by Christ's paschal mystery: in Mary's case it was grace of prevention, in our case it is grace of forgiveness. She was filled from the start with the sanctifying grace normally conferred in baptism. The careful wording of the dogma's promulgation states that since the moment of her conception she was preserved free from all stain of original sin in view of the merits of Jesus Christ. These are the same merits on which we depend.

The Annunciation (25th March)

"Fear not," the angel said. "You shall bring forth a son and call him Jesus." This was a singular mystery (a grace, an action by God), but it had forever been God's intention to establish union with the human race. Therefore the tradition has talked about union with God (divinisation) in terms of inward birth and many Church fathers spoke of the soul corresponding to the Blessed Virgin. Gregory of Nyssa said:

> "What came about in bodily form in Mary…takes place in a similar way in every soul that has been made pure. The Lord does not come in bodily form, for 'we no longer know Christ according to the flesh', but he dwells in us spiritually and the Father takes up his abode with him, the Gospel tells us. In this way the child Jesus is born in each one of us" (*On Virginity*).

The Church is also spoken of as a mother because she has a supernatural fertility, able to birth saints. Augustine says, "Look, mother Church is in labour, see, she is groaning in travail to give birth to you, to bring you forth into the light of faith" (Sermon 216). To ensure this birth of Christ in us is the true function of liturgical times and seasons, prayer and contemplation, sacraments and asceticism.

The Assumption (15th August)

This dogma teaches that Mary, "having completed the course of her earthly life, was assumed body and soul into heavenly glory." This is in keeping with her dignity as the Mother of the Word Incarnate. She is witness to Christ's promise that all Christians will one day be received into paradise. The pathway has been opened from earth to heaven, from the creature to the Creator, from the finite to the Infinite One. Christ blazed that trail when he ascended into heaven, but he intended mankind to follow him. The fact that Mary did is witness to the fact that we can too.

Our redemption involves more than our soul alone. What is assumed is healed, and Jesus took our flesh when he assumed our full humanity - body and soul. He took his flesh from Mary, so now he brings Mary, both body and soul, to heaven. There is no denigration of the body, such as the gnostics taught. This feast contains echoes of the incarnation of Christ and his resurrection of the body, and teaches us what to expect.

Mary became the living tabernacle who housed the Son of God; she now follows the risen Lord to her proper resting-place in heaven. We receive the sacramental Christ in our bodies to prepare them for resurrection.

"The Father in heaven urges us, as children of heaven, to ask for the bread of heaven. [Christ] himself is the bread who, sown in the Virgin, raised up in the flesh, kneaded in the passion, baked in the oven of the tomb, reserved in churches, brought to altars, furnishes the faithful each day with food from heaven." (Peter Chrysologus, quoted in the *Catechism* ¶2837)

Conclusion

We will repeat the liturgical seasons again next year and there is a risk that we will become bored by the repetition. G.K. Chesterton tries to startle us out of this state of mind by suggesting we adopt the mind of a child: "They always say, 'Do it again'; and the grown-up person does it again until he is nearly dead." This repetition comes from a rush of life and he imagines God having this rush of life. The sun rises every day because God never tires of it. "It is possible that God says every morning, 'Do it again' to the sun; and every evening, 'Do it again' to the moon." (*Orthodoxy*) We have sinned, and grown old, and are easily bored, but our Father in heaven is younger than we are. And at every year's end God says, "Do it again," until his Son comes to bring history to its close.

Time moves with a purpose - liturgical time does, anyway (perhaps it is different from worldly time in that way). The purpose of the passage of time is for God to bring us a little closer to himself on shore, bring us a little closer to firm footing on grace, bring us to the mystery he has prepared for us. The mystery is unchanging and eternal but our temporal lives move forward on those eternal waves toward our final end. God has no history but we live in history and time is where our faith unfolds.

Each liturgical year is an annual spiritual track through sin and holiness, death and life, from earth to heaven, from sorrow to beatitude. We are not just examining Jesus' historical steps in the New Testament, we are putting our feet in his footprints and following him to his throne. We are not just remembering his deeds in the past, we are putting on those deeds as our cloak of righteousness. The liturgical year is not a tour through a museum, it brings us further up and further in. Each annual cycle moves us forward, if we would let it.

Further Reading

Adam, A., *The Liturgical Year: Its History and Its Meaning After the Reform of the Liturgy* (Liturgical Press, 1981)

Baldovin, J., and Johnson, M. (eds.), *Between Memory and Hope: Readings on the Liturgical Year* (Liturgical Press, 2001)

Connell, M., *Eternity Today: On the Liturgical Year*, 2 volumes (Continuum, 2006)

Constitution on the Sacred Liturgy (Sacrosanctum Concilium), ch. 5 "The Liturgical Year"

Danielou, J., SJ, *The Bible and the Liturgy* (University of Notre Dame, 2002), ch. 14-19

Heschel, A. J., *The Sabbath* (Farrar Straus Giroux, 2005)

Martimort, A.G., *The Liturgy and Time*, vol. IV of *The Church at Prayer: An Introduction to the Liturgy* (Liturgical Press, 1986)

Nocent, A., *The Liturgical Year*, 4 volumes (Liturgical Press, 2013)

Parsch, P., *The Church's Year of Grace* (Liturgical Press, 1959)

Talley, T. J., *The Origins of the Liturgical Year* (Pueblo Books, 1986)

Universal Norms on the Liturgical Year and the General Roman Calendar (issued by the Sacred Congregation of Rites, 1969)

Music in the Liturgy

Ben Whitworth

There is a growing interest in the ancient musical traditions of the Catholic Church as a support for prayer. This booklet is an introduction for non-specialists, to a fascinating and important topic. It covers the role of music in worship, in the Bible and in the lives of the saints; the theology of music; the history of liturgical music; and the genres of music used at Mass today.

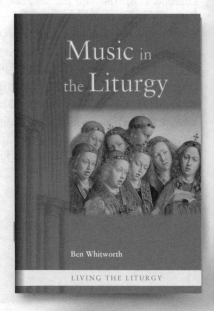

LT05   ISBN 978 1 86082 811 9

Mary in the Liturgy

David W. Fagerberg

The Virgin Mary remained beside Jesus from the manger to the cross - but how does she stay next to Christ and his Church today? Drawing on Church teaching and history, liturgical expert Professor David W. Fagerberg, shows how Mary is central to the life and worship of the Church. She is an example for every Christian in her love for God and accompanies us all on our journey towards Him.

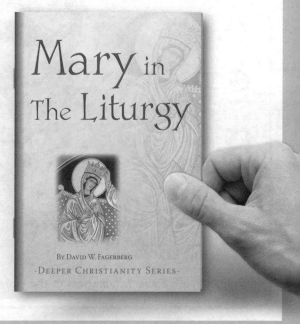

Mary in The Liturgy

By David W. Fagerberg

-Deeper Christianity Series-

SP36   ISBN 978 1 86082 791 4